# THE INCREDIBLE POWER
*in the*

# NAME OF JESUS CHRIST

"And whatsoever ye shall ask in my name, that will I do, that the Father may be glorified in the Son."

**JOHN 14:13**

*By*

**Franklin N. Abazie**

# The incredible power in the name of Jesus Christ
COPYRIGHT 2020 BY Franklin N Abazie
ISBN: 978:1-945-133-94-7

All right reserved. This book or any portion thereof may not be reproduced or used in any manner whatsoever without the express written permission of the publisher, except for the use of brief quotations in a book review. All Bible quotes are from King James Version and others as noted.

**Published by:**
F N ABAZIE PUBLISHING HOUSE---a.k.a,
**Empowerment Bookstore:**

*That I may publish with the voice of thanksgiving and tell of all thy wondrous works.*
**Psalms 26:7**

To order additional copies, wholesales or booking:
Call the Church office (973-372-7518)
or Empowerment Bookstore Hotline 973-393-8518

**Worship address:**
343 Sanford Avenue Newark New Jersey 07106
Administrative Head Office address:
33 Schley Street Newark New Jersey 07112
Email:pastorfranknto@yahoo.com
Website www.fnabaziehealingministries.org
Publishing House: www.fnabaziepublishinghouse.org

This book is a production of F N Abazie
Publishing House. A publication Arms of
Miracle of God Ministries 2020
First Edition

# CONTENTS

The Mandate of The Commission ..................... iv

Arms of The Commission ................................. v

Favor Confession ............................................. vi

Introduction ..................................................... viii

**CHAPTER 1** .................................................. 37
The Supernatural Power in the Name of Jesus

**CHAPTER 2** .................................................. 57
The Power of Deliverance & Protection in
The Name of Jesus

**CHAPTER 3** .................................................. 74
Prayer of Salvation

**CHAPTER 4** .................................................. 84
About The Author

Books By Rev Franklin N Abazie ................... 86

## THE MANDATE OF THE COMMISSION

"THE MOMENT IS DUE TO IMPACT YOUR WORLD THROUGH THE REVIVAL OF THE HEALING & MIRACLE MINISTRY OF JESUS CHRIST OF NAZARETH."

"I AM SENDING YOU TO RESTORE HEALTH UNTO THEE AND I WILL HEAL THEE OF THY WOUNDS, SAID THE LORD OF HOST."

# ARMS OF THE COMMISSION

1) F N Abazie Ministries-Miracle of God Ministries (Miracle Chapel Intl)
2) F N Abazie TV Ministries: Global Television Ministry Outreach.
3) F N Abazie Radio Ministries: Radio Broadcasting Outreach.
4) F N Abazie Publishing House: Book Publication.
5) F N Abazie Bible School: also called Word of Healing Bible School (W.O.H.B.S)
6) F N Abazie Evangelistic Ass: Miracle of God Ministries: Global Crusade
7) Empowerment Bookstore: Book distribution.
8) F N Abazie Helping Hands: Meeting the help of the needy world wide
9) F N Abazie Disaster Recovery Mission: Global Disaster Recovery.
10) F N Abazie Prison Ministry: Prison Ministry for all convicts "Second chance"

**Some of our ministry arms are waiting the appointed time to commence.**

The Incredible Power in The Name of Jesus Christ

# FAVOR CONFESSION

Father thank you for making me righteous and accepted through the blood of Jesus Christ. *Because of that, I am blessed and highly favored by God.* I am the subject of your affection. Your favor surrounds me as a shield, and the first thing that people see around me is your favored shield.

Thank you that I have favor with you and man today. All day long people go out of their way to bless me and help me. *I have favor with everyone that I deal with today. Doors that were once closed are now opened for me.* I receive preferential treatment, and I have special privileges, I am Gods favored child.

No good thing will he withhold from me. Because of Gods favor my enemies cannot triumph over my life. I have supernatural increase and promotion. *I declare restoration to everything that the devil has*

## Favor Confession

*stolen from my life*. I have honor in the midst of my adversaries and an increase in assets, especially in real estate and expansion of territories.

Because I am highly favored by God, I experience great victories, supernatural turnarounds, and miraculous breakthrough in the midst of great impossibilities. *I receive recognition, prominence, and honor. Petitions are granted to me even by ungodly authorities*. Policies, rules, regulations, and laws are changed and reverse on my behalf.

I win battles that I don't even have to fight, because God fights them for me. *This is the day, the set time and the designated moment for me to experience the free favor of God, that profusely and lavishly abound on my behalf in Jesus name.* **Amen.**

# INTRODUCTION

*"If ye shall ask any thing in my name, I will do it."* **John14:14**

I may never get to meet with you in my life time. *But thanks be to God who gave us the opportunity to meet through this medium. "...**but the word of God is not bound.**"* **2timothy2:9.**

It's important to note that "the Name of God" is not only mighty but also a strong tower *"The name of the Lord is a strong tower: the righteous runneth into it, and is safe."* **Proverb18:10.**

My purpose of writing this small book is to share the validity of the Name of Jesus. I like to strongly reaffirm with you that, the *power in the Name of Jesus* is undisputable. Therefore, I will strongly recommend that you approach this small book with *faith,*

## Introduction

*hope, and reverence. The Incredible power in the Name of Jesus is a book designed by the Holy Spirit, for the deliverance of the depressed, the destitute, and the captive.* This *publication is designed to comfort, restore, bring peace, and love.*

This book is written to renew and transform our minds, from every evil thought. I believe as you read and pray, every stronghold will be dismantled. *"And be not conformed to this world: but be ye transformed by the renewing of your mind, that ye may prove what is that good, and acceptable, and perfect, will of God."* **Romans12:2**

Amongst the serval reason for the Name of Jesus is to save his people from their sins. *"And she shall bring forth a son, and thou shalt call his name Jesus: for he shall save his people from their sins."* **Mathew1:21.** May God save us from our sins. May you find peace and love with God in Jesus Mighty Name. **Amen**

Come with me as we examine what the Holy Spirit is saying concerning the incredible power in the Name of Jesus.

Happy reading!

"Whoever loves discipline loves knowledge, but he who hates reproof is stupid."

**Proverb12:1**

As many as I love, I rebuke and chasten: be zealous therefore, and repent.
**Rev 3:19**

"I therefore so run, not as uncertainly; so fight I, not as one that beateth the air:"
**1cor9:26**

"But I keep under my body, and bring it into subjection: lest that by any means, when I have preached to others, I myself should be a castaway."

**1cor9:27**

"I must work the works of him that sent me, while it is day: the night cometh, when no man can work."

**John9:4**

"Whoever spares the rod hates his son, but he who loves him is diligent to discipline him."

**Proverb13:24**

"Those whom I love, I reprove and discipline, so be zealous and repent."
**Revelation 3:19**

"The rod and reproof give wisdom, but a child left to himself brings shame to his mother."

**Proverb29:15**

"So he fed them according to the integrity of his heart; and guided them by the skilfulness of his hands."

**Psalm 78:72**

"And ye have forgotten the exhortation which speaketh unto you as unto children, My son, despise not thou the chastening of the Lord, nor faint when thou art rebuked of him:"

**Hebrews 12:5**

"For whom the Lord loveth he chasteneth, and scourgeth every son whom he receiveth."

**Hebrews 12:6**

"If ye endure chastening, God dealeth with you as with sons; for what son is he whom the father chasteneth not"?

**Hebrews12:7**

"But if ye be without chastisement, whereof all are partakers, then are ye bastards, and not sons."

**Hebrews12:8**

"Furthermore we have had fathers of our flesh which corrected us, and we gave them reverence: shall we not much rather be in subjection unto the Father of spirits, and live?"

**Hebrews12:9**

"He that spareth his rod hateth his son: but he that loveth him chasteneth him betimes."

**Proverb13:24**

"Let thy work appear unto thy servants, and thy glory unto their children."

**Psalm 90:16**

"And let the beauty of the Lord our God be upon us: and establish thou the work of our hands upon us; yea, the work of our hands establish thou it."

**Psalm 90:17**

"And he shall be like a tree planted by the rivers of water, that bringeth forth his fruit in his season; his leaf also shall not wither; and whatsoever he doeth shall prosper."

**Psalm1:3**

"I must work the works of him that sent me, while it is day: the night cometh, when no man can work."

**John9:4**

"For even when we were with you, this we commanded you, that if any would not work, neither should he eat."

**2theo3:10**

xxx

"And that ye study to be quiet, and to do your own business, and to work with your own hands, as we commanded you;
**1theo4:11**

"To discipline a child produces wisdom, but a mother is disgraced by an undisciplined child."

**Proverbs 29:15**

"Whoever loves discipline loves knowledge, but whoever hates correction is stupid."

**Proverbs 12:1**

"Blessed is the one whom God corrects; so do not despise the discipline of the Almighty."
**Job 5:17**

"Blessed is the one you discipline, LORD, the one you teach from your law;"

**Psalm 94:12**

But Jesus answered them, My Father worketh hitherto, and I work.
**John5:17**

# CHAPTER 1

# THE SUPERNATURAL POWER IN THE NAME OF JESUS

*"Then Peter said, Silver and gold have I none; but such as I have give I thee: In the name of Jesus Christ of Nazareth rise up and walk."* **Acts 3:6**

I am so excited to talk to you a little more about the supernatural power in the Name of Jesus. You see! There is power in the Name of Jesus. Hear me…

There is no other name that can save anyone but the Name of Jesus Christ. "*Neither is there salvation in any other: for there is none other name under heaven given among men, whereby we must be saved.*" **Acts 4:12**

When Philip went to Samaria, he preached only that name –Christ. "*Then*

*Philip went down to the city of Samaria, and preached Christ unto them."* **Acts8:5**

When you know his name He manifests his Power unto you. *"But as many as received him, to them gave he power to become the sons of God, even to them that believe on his name".***John1:12**

That means when you believe in Jesus Christ, the Son of God, you have life in His name. (John 20:31). There is, in fact, no other name under heaven given among men whereby we can be saved (Acts 4:12). So, naturally, whatever we do, in word or deed, we ought to do in the name of the Lord Jesus (Col. 3:17).

"God has highly exalted him and bestowed on him the name that is above every name, so that at the name of Jesus every knee should bow, in heaven and on earth and under the earth, and every tongue

## Chapter 1: The Supernatural Power in the Name of Jesus

confess that Jesus Christ is Lord, to the glory of God the Father" (Phil. 2:9–11).

*"Hitherto have ye asked nothing in my name: ask, and ye shall receive, that your joy may be full."* **John 16:24**

*There is great power in the Name of Jesus.* This supernatural power only manifests to us who know how to apply it. There are people who call on his Name and yet disobey God in their actions in life. *And why call ye me, Lord, Lord, and do not the things which I say?*

**For His Name to manifest his power upon your life you must live by faith.** *"But without faith it is impossible to please him: for he that cometh to God must believe that he is, and that he is a rewarder of them that diligently seek him."* **Hebrews 11:6**

We were told…….

"Yea, a man may say, Thou hast faith, and I have works: shew me thy faith without thy works, and I will shew thee my faith by my works." **James2:18**

"For as the body without the spirit is dead, so faith without works is dead also." **James2:26.**

So, a life of faith is a life of victory. If you live by faith, you will experience the supernatural power in the Name of Jesus.

Secondly, you must live a Holy life

**You must live a holy live acceptable to God.** "*I beseech you therefore, brethren, by the mercies of God, that ye present your bodies a living sacrifice, holy, acceptable unto God, which is your reasonable service.*" **Romans12:1**

***Holiness is the key to victory over every work of the devil.*** He that committeth sin is of the devil; for the devil sinneth from the

## Chapter 1: The Supernatural Power in the Name of Jesus

beginning. For this purpose the Son of God was manifested, that he might destroy the works of the devil. **1 John 3:8**

*"And declared to be the Son of God with power, according to the spirit of holiness, by the resurrection from the dead:"* **Romans 1:4**

**Whenever you live a holy lifestyle you are pure in the heart**. My bible says *"Blessed are the pure in heart: for they shall see God".* **Mathew 5:8**

Holiness as a lifestyle, enables us to do great things in the kingdom of God-*what do I mean?* If you know God you must develop faith unconsciously. If you live a holy life, you are totally free from all immoralities.

"Now the works of the flesh are manifest, which are these; Adultery, fornication, uncleanness, lasciviousness, Idolatry, witchcraft, hatred, variance, emulations, wrath, strife, seditions, heresies,

Envyings, murders, drunkenness, revellings, and such like:…" **Gal5:22**

**It takes a lifestyle of holiness to destroy all work of the flesh as established in the above scripture.**

**Remember** ….."*Faith worketh by love."* Gal 5:6

**If you know God you will do exploits.** *And such as do wickedly against the covenant shall he corrupt by flatteries: but the people that do know their God shall be strong, and do exploits.*

If you desire his power you must learn to pray often. "*And he spake a parable unto them to this end, that men ought always to pray, and not to faint."* **Luke18:1**

The *lifestyle of prayer* attracts His *ever abiding presence. In His presence is fullness of joy.* That presence grants signs and wonder to be done by the name of thy

## Chapter 1: The Supernatural Power in the Name of Jesus

holy child Jesus. *"And now, Lord, behold their threatenings: and grant unto thy servants, that with all boldness they may speak thy word, By stretching forth thine hand to heal; and that signs and wonders may be done by the name of thy holy child Jesus."* **Acts 4:29-30**

"And these signs shall follow them that believe; In my name shall they cast out devils; they shall speak with new tongues;" **Mark 16:17**

"And whatsoever ye shall ask in my name, that will I do, that the Father may be glorified in the Son. If ye shall ask any thing in my name, I will do it." **John 14:13-14**.

Jesus promised us as the mediator that whatever we ask in His Name, He will do it. *And whatsoever ye do in word or deed, do all in the name of the Lord Jesus, giving thanks to God and the Father by him.* **Col 3:17**

**If you know Him, you must know His Name, and how to use His Name**. "And these signs shall follow them that believe; In my name shall they cast out devils; they shall speak with new tongues;" Mark16:17

*"But I know him: for I am from him, and he hath sent me."* **John7:29**

*"Yet ye have not known him; but I know him: and if I should say, I know him not, I shall be a liar like unto you: but I know him, and keep his saying."* **John8:55**

**If you know Him, you must use His Name wisely.** Yet ye have not known him; but I know him: and if I should say, I know him not, I shall be a liar like unto you: but I know him, and keep his saying.

Whenever you understand how to represent His name, you become *an ambassador for His Power and Presence*. God is too faithful to fail. If you depend upon God, you will never be disappointed

**Chapter 1**: The Supernatural Power in the Name of Jesus

in life. But if you depend on man, you will forever always suffer disappointment, delay, and setbacks.

## 50 Names of Jesus:

For to us a child is born, to us a son is given, and the government will be on his shoulders. And he will be called Wonderful Counselor, Mighty God, Everlasting Father, Prince of Peace." **Is. 9:6**

1. **Almighty One** – "…who is and who was and who is to come, the Almighty." Rev. 1:8

2. **Alpha and Omega** – "I am the Alpha and the Omega, the First and the Last, the Beginning and the End." Rev. 22:13

3. **Advocate** – "My dear children, I write this to you so that you will not sin. But if anybody does sin, we have

an advocate with the Father--Jesus Christ, the Righteous One." 1 John 2:1

4. **Author and Perfecter of Our Faith** – "Fixing our eyes on Jesus, the author and perfecter of faith, who for the joy set before Him endured the cross, despising the shame, and has sat down at the right hand of the throne of God." Heb. 12:2

5. **Authority** – "Jesus said, 'All authority in heaven and on earth has been given to me." Matt. 28:18

6. **Bread of Life** – "Then Jesus declared, 'I am the bread of life. Whoever comes to me will never go hungry, and whoever believes in me will never be thirsty.'" John 6:35

7. **Beloved Son of God** – "And behold, a voice from heaven said, "This is my beloved Son, with whom I am well pleased." Matt. 3:17

8. **Bridegroom** – "And Jesus said to them, "Can the wedding guests mourn as long as the bridegroom is with them? The days will come when the bridegroom is taken away from them, and then they will fast." Matt. 9:15

9. **Chief Cornerstone** – "The stone which the builders rejected has become the chief corner stone." Ps. 118:22

10. **Deliverer** – "And to wait for his Son from heaven, whom he raised from the dead, Jesus who delivers us from the wrath to come." 1 Thess.1:10

11. **Faithful and True** – "I saw heaven standing open and there before me was a white horse, whose rider is called Faithful and True. With justice he judges and wages war." Rev.19:11

12. **Good Shepherd** - "I am the good shepherd. The good shepherd lays down his life for the sheep." John 10:11

13. **Great High Priest** – "Therefore, since we have a great high priest who has passed through the heavens, Jesus the Son of God, let us hold fast our confession." Heb. 4:14

14. **Head of the Church** – "And he put all things under his feet and gave him as head over all things to the church." Eph. 1:22

15. **Holy Servant** – "…and grant that Your bond-servants may speak Your word with all confidence, while You extend Your hand to heal, and signs and wonders take place through the name of Your holy servant Jesus." Acts 4:29-30

## Chapter 1: The Supernatural Power in the Name of Jesus

16. **I am** – "Jesus said to them, "Truly, truly, I say to you, before Abraham was, I am." John 8:58

17. **Immanuel** – "…She will give birth to a son and will call him Immanuel, which means 'God with us.'" Is. 7:14

18. **Indescribable Gift** – "Thanks be to God for His indescribable gift." 2 Cor. 9:15

19. **Judge** – "…he is the one whom God appointed as judge of the living and the dead." Acts 10:42

20. **King of Kings** – "These will wage war against the Lamb, and the Lamb will overcome them, because He is Lord of lords and King of kings, and those who are with Him are the called and chosen and faithful." Rev. 17:14

21. **Lamb of God** – "The next day John saw Jesus coming toward him and

said, "Look, the Lamb of God, who takes away the sin of the world!" John 1:29

22. **Light of the World** – "I am the light of the world. Whoever follows me will never walk in darkness, but will have the light of life." John 8:12

23. **Lion of the Tribe of Judah** – "Weep no more; behold, the Lion of the tribe of Judah, the Root of David, has conquered, so that he can open the scroll and its seven seals." Rev. 5:5

24. **Lord of All** – "For this reason also, God highly exalted Him, and bestowed on Him the name which is above every name, so that at the name of Jesus every knee will bow, of those who are in heaven and on earth and under the earth, and that every tongue will confess that Jesus Christ is Lord,

**Chapter 1**: The Supernatural Power in the Name of Jesus

to the glory of God the Father." Phil. 2:9-11

**25. Mediator** – "For there is one God, and one mediator between God and men, the man Christ Jesus." 1 Tim. 2:5

**26. Messiah** – "We have found the Messiah" (that is, the Christ)." John 1:41

**27. Mighty One** – "Then you will know that I, the Lord, am your Savior, your Redeemer, the Mighty One of Jacob." Is. 60:16

**28. One Who Sets Free** – "So if the Son sets you free, you will be free indeed." John 8:36

**29. Our Hope** – "…Christ Jesus our hope." 1 Tim. 1:1

**30. Peace** – "For he himself is our peace, who has made the two groups one and has destroyed the barrier, the dividing wall of hostility," Eph. 2:14

31. **Prophet** – "And Jesus said to them, "A prophet is not without honor, except in his hometown and among his relatives and in his own household." Mark 6:4

32. **Redeemer** – "And as for me, I know that my Redeemer lives, and at the last He will take His stand on the earth." Job 19:25

33. **Risen Lord** – "…that Christ died for our sins according to the Scriptures, that he was buried, that he was raised on the third day according to the Scriptures." 1 Cor. 15:3-4

34. **Rock** – "For they drank from the spiritual Rock that followed them, and the Rock was Christ." 1 Cor. 10:4

## Chapter 1: The Supernatural Power in the Name of Jesus

**35. Sacrifice for Our Sins** – "This is love: not that we loved God, but that he loved us and sent his Son as an atoning sacrifice for our sins." 1 John 4:10

**36. Savior** – "For unto you is born this day in the city of David a Savior, who is Christ the Lord." Luke 2:11

**37. Son of Man** – "For the Son of Man came to seek and to save the lost." Luke 19:10

**38. Son of the Most High** – "He will be great and will be called the Son of the Most High. The Lord God will give him the throne of his father David." Luke 1:32

**39. Supreme Creator Over All** – "By Him all things were created, both in the heavens and on earth, visible and invisible, whether thrones or dominions or rulers or authorities--

all things have been created through Him and for Him. He is before all things, and in Him all things hold together...." Col. 1:16-17

40. **Resurrection and the Life** – "Jesus said to her, "I am the resurrection and the life. The one who believes in me will live, even though they die." John 11:25

41. **The Door** – "I am the door. If anyone enters by me, he will be saved and will go in and out and find pasture." John 10:9

42. **The Way** – "Jesus answered, "I am the way and the truth and the life. No one comes to the Father except through me." John 14:6

43. **The Word** – "In the beginning was the Word, and the Word was with God, and the Word was God." John 1:1

44. **True Vine** - "I am the true vine, and My Father is the vinedresser." John 15:1

45. **Truth** – "And you will know the truth, and the truth will set you free." John 8:32

46. **Victorious One** – "To the one who is victorious, I will give the right to sit with me on my throne, just as I was victorious and sat down with my Father on his throne." Rev. 3:21

47. **Wonderful Counselor**,

48. **Mighty God**,

49. **Everlasting Father**,

50. **Prince of Peace** – "For to us a child is born, to us a son is given, and the government will be on his shoulders. And he will be called Wonderful Counselor, Mighty God, Everlasting Father, Prince of Peace." Is. 9:6

# The Incredible Power in The Name of Jesus Christ

GOD
ROCK
SAVIOR
MESSIAH
IMMANUEL
HOLY • CHILD
MIGHTY • GOD
LORD • OF • ALL
LAMB • OF • GOD
CHRIST • OF • GOD
KING • OF • KINGS
THE • WORD • OF • GOD
ALPHA • AND • OMEGA
PRINCE • OF • PEACE
LIGHT • OF • THE • WORLD
HEAD • OF • THE • CHURCH
SON • OF • THE • HIGHEST
EVERLASTING • FATHER
RESURRECTION • AND • LIFE
JESUS

## CHAPTER 2

**THE POWER OF DELIVERANCE & PROTECTION IN THE NAME OF JESUS**

"He shall call upon me, and I will answer him: I will be with him in trouble; I will deliver him, and honour him." **Psalm 91:15**

*"Call unto me, and I will answer thee, and show thee great and mighty things, which thou knowest not."* **Jer 33:3**

Often most people plead the blood of Jesus Christ whenever they find themselves in trouble or in a trial. There is a prevailing power in the blood of Jesus. One of the reasons for the finished work of the cross on Calvary, is our constant protection and deliverance from the trap of the devil. *For he shall give his angels charge over thee, to keep thee in all thy ways.*

## GODS PRESENCE PROTECTS US FROM EVIL

"I will say of the Lord, He is my refuge and my fortress: my God; in him will I trust. Surely he shall deliver thee from the snare of the fowler, and from the noisome pestilence. He shall cover thee with his feathers, and under his wings shalt thou trust: his truth shall be thy shield and buckler. "**Psalms91:2-4**

"Thou shalt not be afraid for the terror by night; nor for the arrow that flieth by day; Nor for the pestilence that walketh in darkness; nor for the destruction that wasteth at noonday. A thousand shall fall at thy side, and ten thousand at thy right hand; but it shall not come nigh thee."**Psalm91:5-7**

**Chapter 2** : The Power of Deliverance

We see the Power of God when He divided the red sea for Moses and the people of Israel escaped from the wicked hand of pharaoh. *"And he said, My presence shall go with thee, and I will give thee rest."*

David said *"I will take the cup of salvation, and call upon the name of the Lord."* Psalm116:13

*"Then called I upon the name of the Lord; O Lord, I beseech thee, deliver my soul."* **Psalm116:4**

**God anoints anyone of his people liberally and freely.** "For *the gifts and calling of God are without repentance."* **Romans11:29.**

It is by grace and not by merit. *"So then it is not of him that willeth, nor of him that runneth, but of God that sheweth mercy."* **Romans9:16**

*"But when it pleased God, who separated me from my mother's womb, and called me by his grace."* **Gal1:15**

**"Whatsoever the Lord pleased, that did he in heaven, and in earth, in the seas, and all deep places." Psalm135:6**

*"But our God is in the heavens: he hath done whatsoever he hath pleased."* **Psalm115:3**

# HOW TO USE THE NAME OF JESUS

1. We use the Name of Jesus to Put Sickness to Flight. "In my name… they will lay hands on the sick, and they will recover." – Mark 16:17-18 (NKJV)

2. We use the Name of Jesus to Rebuke Lack. "Therefore, God elevated him to the place of highest honor and gave

**Chapter 2** : The Power of Deliverance

him the name above all other names, that at the name of Jesus every knee should bow, in heaven and on earth and under the earth."

3. We use the Name of Jesus to evict evil spirits. "In My name they will cast out demons." – Mark 16:17 (NKJV)

4. We use the Name of Jesus for Supernatural Protection. *"The name of the Lord is a strong tower: the righteous runneth into it, and is safe."* Proverb18:10

# MANIFESTATION OF POWER IN THE NAME OF JESUS

### 1. Devil become impotent in His Name

"And the seventy returned again with joy, saying, Lord, even the devils are subject unto us through thy name." **Luke10:17**

## 2. The demons were cast out in his name

"And these signs shall follow them that believe; In my name shall they cast out devils; they shall speak with new tongues;" **Mark 16:17**

## 3. Healing manifests in his name.

"Then Peter said, Silver and gold have I none; but such as I have give I thee: In the name of Jesus Christ of Nazareth rise up and walk. And he took him by the right hand, and lifted him up: and immediately his feet and ankle bones received strength." **Acts3:6-7**

## 4. Salvation comes in his name

"Neither is there salvation in any other: for there is none other name under heaven given among men, whereby we must be saved." **Acts4:12**

**Chapter 2** : The Power of Deliverance

## 5. We are to baptize in his name

"Go ye therefore, and teach all nations, baptizing them in the name of the Father, and of the Son, and of the Holy Ghost:" **Mathew28:19.**

## 6. We are justified in his name

"And such were some of you: but ye are washed, but ye are sanctified, but ye are justified in the name of the Lord Jesus, and by the Spirit of our God." **1 Cor. 6:11.**

## 7. We are commanded to do everything we do in his name.

"And whatsoever ye do in word or deed, do all in the name of the Lord Jesus, giving thanks to God and the Father by him." **Col3:17**

*What does it mean to pray in the name of Jesus?*

1. *By calling on His Name, we humble our self and submit to His sovereignty.* His

Name grants us access into supernatural things in life.

2. *We identify with the person of Jesus Christ.*

Jesus has literally given us his name. When I use that name, I am confessing that he is mine and that I am his. It is like going to the bank of heaven, knowing I have nothing deposited. If I go in my name I will get absolutely nothing. But Jesus Christ has unlimited funds in heaven's bank, and he has granted me the privilege of going to the bank with his name on my checks.

3. *We pray in his authority.*

The Name of Jesus comes with authority. If you call upon His name, you call upon his authority.

4. *We submit to his will.*

When we call in his Name we submit to his will and His authority. "And he said

## Chapter 2 : The Power of Deliverance

unto them, When ye pray, say, Our Father which art in heaven, Hallowed be thy name. Thy kingdom come. Thy will be done, as in heaven, so in earth." **Luke 11:2**

5. *We are representing him and his interests here on earth.*

It is much the same as the legal arrangement known as the power of attorney. In such matters one person may represent another in his absence. They act in their behalf. Jesus has given every believer unlimited and general power of attorney in all matters and with the right to use his name in every situation.

6. *We pray expectantly.*

When we pray in Jesus' name, we may expect the answer in accord with the value of his name. So we can pray with great expectation.

# HINDRANCES TO THE AUTHORITY IN THE NAME OF JESUS

----------- *IDOL WORSHIP* -------------

"Thou shalt not take the name of the Lord thy God in vain; for the Lord will not hold him guiltless that taketh his name in vain." **Exodus20:7**

---*DOUBT OF THE POWER IN THE NAME OF JESUS*---

*"A double minded man is unstable in all his ways."* **James1:8**

Doubting the Power in the Name of Jesus, means you do not believe in His Power and His Presence. Any unbelief is not of God.

--------What we should do--------

**Reverence His Name**

**Chapter 2** : The Power of Deliverance

*"He sent redemption unto his people: he hath commanded his covenant for ever: holy and reverend is his name."* **Psalm111:9**

**Pray in His Name**

**Jesus is the access way to the Father.**

*"And whatsoever ye shall ask in my name, that will I do, that the Father may be glorified in the Son. If ye shall ask any thing in my name, I will do it."* **John14:13-14**

"Hitherto have ye asked nothing in my name: ask, and ye shall receive, that your joy may be full." **John16:24**

*"Therefore the Lord himself shall give you a sign; Behold, a virgin shall conceive, and bear a son, and shall call his name Immanuel."* **Isa7:14**

*"For unto us a child is born, unto us a son is given: and the government shall be upon his shoulder: and his name shall be called Wonderful, Counsellor, The mighty*

*God, The everlasting Father, The Prince of Peace."* **Isaiah9:6**

There is Power in the Name of Jesus. Send us your prayer request and let's continue to intercede for you and your family and business

# WE WANT TO HEAR FROM YOU. PLEASE TAKE TIME TO WRITE ME BACK

**Rev Franklin N Abazie**

33 Schley street Newark New Jersey 07112.
I want to keep you in my prayers send me your prayer request

**MIRACLE OF GOD MINISTRIES INC**

343 Sanford avenue Newark
New Jersey 07106

Also send in your generous donation to support this work at
www.fnabaziehealingministries.org

## Conclusion

*"But as many as received him, to them gave he power to become the sons of God, even to them that believe on his name."* **John1:12**

Amongst our mission for writing this small book is to convert unbelievers to believe in His name. I do not know where you stand but the word says ….

**"Therefore if any man be in Christ, he is a new creature: old things are passed away; behold, all things are become new". 2cor5:17**

*I encourage you to repent in prayers of any negative word you have ever spoken against your life and future. Speak the right word and make these confessions boldly in faith.*

**Chapter 2** : The Power of Deliverance

# REPEAT THIS PRAYER AFTER ME....

*"Say Lord Jesus, I accept you today, as my Lord and my savior, forgive me of my sins wash me with your blood. Right now, I believe, I am sanctified. I am save. I am free. I am free from the Power of sin to serve the Lord Jesus. Thank you Lord for saving me. Amen."*

What must I do to determine my divine visitation?

To determine divine visitation you must be born again!

*The word says as many as received him, to them gave He power to become the sons of God. Even to them that believe on his name.*

To qualify for divine visitation do the following sincerely

1) Acknowledge that you are a sinner and that He died for you. Rom3:23.

2) Repent of your sins. Acts 3:19, Luke13:5, 2Peter3:9

3) Believe in your heart that Jesus died for your sin. Romans10:10

4) Confess Jesus as the Lord over your life. Romans10:10, Acts2:21

I really want to hear from you. You can join me if you are in the area to worship with us

# MIRACLE OF GOD MINISTRIES INC

343 SANFORD AVENUE NEWARK
NEW JERSEY 07106
Jesus is Lord!

EMAIL: Pastorfranknto@yahoo.com
Website www.fnabaziehealingministries.org

Please feel free to write me

**REV FRANKLIN N ABAZIE**
33 Schley street Newark
New Jersey 07112

# CHAPTER 3

## PRAYER OF SALVATION

"Neither is there salvation in any other: for there is none other name under heaven given among men, whereby we must be saved." **Acts4:12**

There is only one name that will take us into heaven.

What must I do to determine my salvation?

To be saved-*we must be born again!*
---*Then dream big and believe in your self*

To qualify for divine visitation do the following sincerely

1) Acknowledge that you are a sinner and that He died for you. Rom3:23.

2) Repent of your sins. Acts 3:19, Luke13:5, 2Peter3:9

**Chapter 3** : Prayer of Salvation

3) Believe in your heart that Jesus died for your sin. Romans 10:10

4) Confess Jesus as the Lord over your life. Romans 10:10, Acts 2:21

### *Are you saved?*

If God have saved your life, speak to someone about Jesus. Disciple someone to join you worship the Lord Jesus Christ.

## MIRACLE CARE OUTREACH

**"...But that the members should have the same care one for another" 1cor12:25**

We are all members of the body of Christ. Jesus commanded us to love our neighbor as ourselves. This includes caring for one another as a member of one body. True love is expressed in caring and giving. The word says for God so Love He gave....

Reach out to someone in need of Jesus, help someone in crisis find Christ. Look out and prove your love to Jesus by caring and inviting your friends and associates to find Jesus the Healer.

Invite your friends to our Home Care Cell Fellowship (Miracle chapel Intl Satellite fellowship) In the USA at 33 Schley Street Newark New Jersey 07112.

If you are in Nigeria—
**MIRACLE OF GOD MINISTRIES**

A.K.A **"MIRACLE CHAPEL INTL"**
Mpama –Egbu-Owerri Imo state Nigeria.

(Home Care Cell fellowship Group).
We meet every Tuesday at 6:00pm-7:00pm.

# LIFE IS NOT ALL ABOUT DURATION BUT ITS ALL ABOUT DONATION

*What does the above statement mean? ....*

## Chapter 3 : Prayer of Salvation

Life consists not in accumulation of material wealth. (Luke12:15) But it's all about liberality….meaning- what you can give and share with others. Proverb11:25.

When you live for others--You live forever- You out live your generation by the legacy you live behind after you depart into glory to be with the Lord.

But when you live to yourself - you are reduced to self—you are easily forgotten when you die and depart in glory. Permit me to admonish you today to live your life to be a blessing to a soul connected to you today.

I want you to know that so many souls are connected and looking up to you, and through you so many souls will be saved and rescued from destruction. Will you disciple someone today to find Jesus Christ?

As a genuine Christian; it is your duty to evangelize Jesus Christ to all you meet on your way. Jesus is still in the healing business-Jesus is still doing miracles from time of old to now. Therefore tell someone about Jesus Christ today, disciple and bring them to Church. John 1:45 *Philip findeth Nathanael....*

Please to prove the sincerity of your love for God today; please become a soul winner. The dignity of your Christianity is hidden in your boldness to proclaim and evangelize Jesus Christ to all you meet on your way.

There is a question mark on the integrity of your Christianity until you become a life soul winner. Invite someone to join us worship the Lord Jesus this coming Sunday. Amen

**Chapter 3** : Prayer of Salvation

# MIRACLE OF GOD MINISTRIES PILLARS OF THE COMMISSION

We Believe Preach and Practice the following

1) We believe and preach Salvation to every living human being

2) We believe and preach Repentance and forgiveness of sins

3) We believe and preach the baptism of the Holy Spirit and Spiritual gifts

4) We believe and teach the Prosperity

5) We believe and preach Divine Healing and Miracles (Signs &Wonder)

6) We believe and preach Faith

7) We believe and Proclaim the Power of God (Supernatural)

8) We believe and Proclaim Praise& Worship to God

9) We believe and preach Wisdom

10) We believe and preach Holiness (Consecration)

11) We believe and preach Vision

12) We believe and teach the Word of God

13) We believe and teach Success

14) We believe and practice Prayer

15) We believe and teach Deliverance

**This 15 stones form the Pillars of Our Commission.** Become part of this church family and follow this great move of God.

## MY HEART FELT PRAYER FOR YOU

It is my prayer that you dream big and believe in yourself. I see you impacting your world. I see you making a difference. I see you breaking through. I see the Glory of God upon your life.

**Chapter 3** : Prayer of Salvation

***Now let me Pray for you:***

My Father, My Father, Grant me the ability to *Dream big and believe in myself* in the Mighty Name of Jesus Christ.

# THE POWER OF EVANGELISM

"Go ye therefore, and teach all nations, baptizing them in the name of the Father, and of the Son, and of the Holy Ghost:" **Mathew28:19**

Evangelism has power to attract the blessing of the Lord upon our lives. It is written "And ye shall serve the Lord your God, and he shall bless thy bread, and thy water; and I will take sickness away from the midst of thee." Exodus23:26.

Evangelizing, and bringing men and women to the cross of Jesus Christ is a great commandment. According to the above scripture, we are commanded to teach all nations, the name of Jesus Christ.

It is my prayer that you will witness the name of Jesus Christ to someone today.

*Remember…………*

*"And they that be wise shall shine as the brightness of the firmament; and they that turn many to righteousness as the stars for ever and ever."* **Daniel 12:3**

# OPERATION--"ONE MAN TEN MEN"

*"Thus saith the Lord of hosts; In those days it shall come to pass, that ten men shall take hold out of all languages of the nations, even shall take hold of the skirt of him that is a Jew, saying, We will go with you: for we have heard that God is with you."* **Zech 8:23**

If someone directed you to this ministry, it is divine wisdom for you to bring someone else also. If you googled to come into contact with us, I will recommend you also

## Chapter 3 : Prayer of Salvation

tell ten of your contacts and share with them what Jesus is doing through this ministry. Tell everybody about Jesus, also tell them to contact this ministry. Jesus is Lord!!

# OPERATION ONE MAN ONE SOUL

If you cannot bring ten people at one time, at least you can talk to one person per time.

I recommend that you look for just one person who will respond positively and bring them to church. Or tell them about this ministry. That convert, is your own convert minister to them the love of Jesus Christ.

**JESUS IS LORD!**

# CHAPTER 4
## ABOUT THE AUTHOR

Rev Franklin N Abazie is the founding and Presiding Pastor of Miracle of God Ministries with headquarters in Newark, New Jersey USA and a branch church in Owerri- Imo State Nigeria. He is following the footsteps of one of his mentors, Oral Roberts (Healing Evangelist) of the blessed memory. The Lord passed Oral Roberts healing mantle two days before he went to be with the Lord at age 91 into the hand of healing evangelist-Rev Franklin N Abazie in a vision.

In all his services the Power and Presence of God is present to heal all in his audience. He is an ordained man of God with a Healing Ministry reviving the healing and miracle ministry of Jesus Christ of Nazareth.

## Chapter 4 : About The Author

Pastor Franklin N Abazie, is called by God with a unique mandate: **"THE MOMENT IS DUE TO IMPACT YOUR WORLD THROUGH THE REVIVAL OF THE HEALING & MIRACLE MINISTRY OF JESUS CHRIST OF NAZARETH**

**I AM SENDING YOU TO RESTORE HEALTH UNTO THEE AND I WILL HEAL THEE OF THY WOUNDS. SAID THE LORD OF HOST"**

He is a gifted ardent Teacher of the word of God who operates also in the office of a Prophet, generating and attracting undeniable signs & wonders, special miracles and healings, with apostolic fireworks of the Holy Ghost. He is the founding and presiding senior Pastor of this fast growing Healing ministry. He has written over 86 inspirational, healing and transforming books covering almost all aspect of divine healing and life. He is happily married and blessed with children.

# BOOKS BY REV FRANKLIN N ABAZIE

1) Commanding Abundance
2) The outcome of faith
3) Understanding the secret of prevailing prayers.
4) Understanding the secret of the man God uses
5) Activating my due Season
6) Overcoming Divine Verdicts
7) The Outcome of Divine Wisdom
8) Understanding God's Restoration Mandate
9) Walking in the Victory and Authority of the truth
10) Gods Covenant Exemption
11) Destiny Restoration Pillars

## Books By Rev Franklin N Abazie

12) Provoking Acceptable Praise
13) Understanding Divine Judgment
14) Activating Angelic Re-enforcement
15) Provoking Un-Merited Favor
16) The Benefits of the Speaking faith
17) Understanding Divine Arrangement
18) Understanding Divine Healing
19) The Mystery of Endurance
20) Obeying Divine Instructions
21) Understanding the Voice of God
22) Never give up on Hope
23) The prevailing Power of faith
24) Understanding Divine Prosperity
25) The Reward of Prayer
26) Covenant Keys to Answered Prayers
27) Activating the Forces of Vengeance

28) Put your faith to work
29) Where is your trust?
30) The Audacity of the Blood of Jesus
31) Redeeming Your Days
32) The Force of Vision
33) Breaking the shackles of Family curses
34) Wisdom for Marriage Stability
35) Overcoming prevailing challenges
36) The Prayer solution
39) The power of Prayer
40) Prayer strategy
41) The prayer that works
42) Walking in Forgiveness
43) The Power of the grace of God
44) The Power of Persistence

45) Overcoming Divine verdicts
46) The benefit of the speaking faith.
47) Fearless faith
48) Redeeming Your Days.
49) The Supernatural Power of Prophecy
50) The companionship of the Holy Spirit
51) Understanding Divine Judgement
52) Understanding Divine Prosperity
53) Dominating Controlling Forces
54) The winner's Faith
55) Destiny Restoration Pillars
56) Developing Spiritual Muscles
57) Inexplicable faith
58) The lifestyle of Prayer
59) Developing a positive attitude in life.
60) The Mystery of Divine supply

61) Encounter with the Power of God
62) Walking in love
63) Praying in the Spirit
64) How to provoke your testimony
65) Walking in the reality of the anointing
66) The Reality of new birth
67) The Price of freedom
68) The Supernatural Power of faith
69) The intellectual components of Redemption.
70) Overcoming Fear
71) Overcoming Prevailing Challenges
72) My life & Ministry
73) The Mystery of Praise
74) Dream Big and believe in yourself

Books By Rev Franklin N Abazie

**75)** The Incredible Power in the Name of Jesus

**76)** The Power of Bold Declaration

**77)** The Power of Discipline & Dedication

# MIRACLE OF GOD MINISTRIES

*NIGERIA CRUSADE*
*2012*

**MIRACLE OF GOD MINISTRIES**

*NIGERIA CRUSADE 2012*

# MIRACLE OF GOD MINISTRIES

*NIGERIA CRUSADE
2012*

> ¹But now thus saith the LORD that created thee, O Jacob, and he that formed thee, O Israel, Fear not: for I have redeemed thee, I have called thee by thy name; thou art mine.
>
> Isaiah 43:1 KJV

www.ingramcontent.com/pod-product-compliance
Lightning Source LLC
Chambersburg PA
CBHW030158100526
44592CB00009B/331